Little Creatures

Honeybees

by Lisa J. Amstutz

a Capstone company — publishers for children

Raintree is an imprint of Capstone Global Library Limited, a company incorporated in England and Wales having its registered office at 264 Banbury Road, Oxford, OX2 7DY – Registered company number: 6695582

www.raintree.co.uk
myorders@raintree.co.uk

Text © Capstone Global Library Limited 2018
The moral rights of the proprietor have been asserted.

Edited by Gena Chester
Designed by Sarah Bennett
Picture research by Wanda Winch
Production by Tori Abraham
Originated by Capstone Global Library Limited
Printed and bound in China

ISBN 978 1 4747 4254 2
21 20 19 18 17
10 9 8 7 6 5 4 3 2 1

British Library Cataloguing in Publication Data
A full catalogue record for this book is available from the British Library.

Acknowledgements
We would like to thank the following for permission to reproduce photographs:
Dreamstime: Inventori, 11; Shutterstock: Maciej Olszewski, cover, Barsan ATTILA, 15, Billion Photos, 3, 24, Daniel Prudek, 7, Darios, 17, Fotopb.peter, 22, Mirko Graul, 19, 21, muratart, 1, NattyPTG, meadow background, Serg64, 5, szefei, 13, Who What When Where Why Wector, 9

Every effort has been made to contact copyright holders of material reproduced in this book. Any omissions will be rectified in subsequent printings if notice is given to the publisher.

Contents

Busy bees

Buzz!

There goes a honeybee!

It is looking for food.

Honeybees are insects.

They have six legs.

They have three main
body parts.

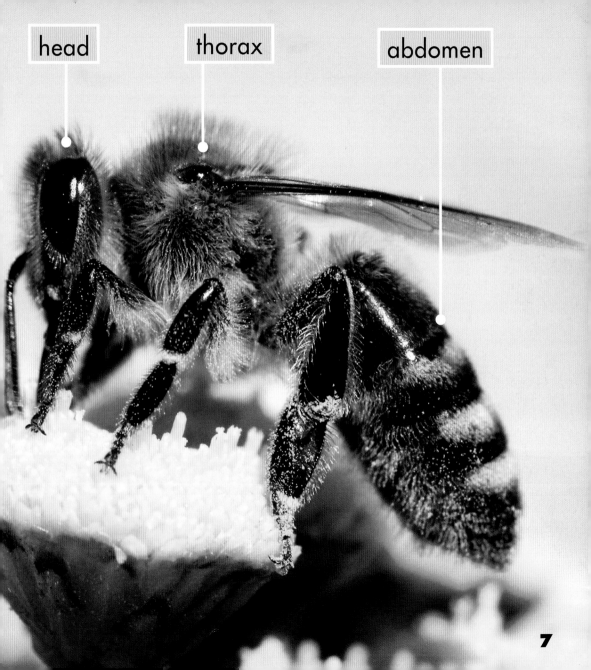

head

thorax

abdomen

7

Bees live in a hive.

They have many jobs to do.

The hive is always busy.

Ouch!

Most bees can sting.

They keep the hive safe.

Sweet as honey

Bees fly to flowers.

Slurp!

They sip nectar.

It is sweet.

The bees fly home.

They put nectar in the hive.

It turns into honey.

Bees eat honey in winter.

People like to eat it too.

Yum!

Growing up

A queen bee lays eggs.

Larvae hatch out.

They look like worms.

larvae

A cocoon covers each larva.

Soon a new bee comes out.

It starts working right away.

new bee

20

Glossary

cocoon covering made of silky thread; some insects make a cocoon to protect themselves while they change from larvae to pupae

hive place where a colony of bees lives; thousands of bees live in one hive

honey sweet, sticky substance that honeybees make from nectar

insect small animal with a hard outer shell, six legs, three body sections and two antennae; most insects have wings

larva insect at the stage of development between an egg and an adult

nectar sweet liquid found in many flowers

Find out more

Egg to Bee (Lifecycles), Camilla De La Bedoyere, (QED, 2016)

Flight of the Honey Bee (Nature Storybooks), Raymond Huber (Walker, 2013)

Life Cycle of a Honey Bee, Grace Jones (Book Life, 2015)

Websites

www.bbc.co.uk/education/clips/zhgd2hv
Learn about different kinds of bees and the jobs they do as well as how they make honey and store it.

www.ngkids.co.uk/animals/Honey-Bees
Discover ten facts about honeybees.

Critical thinking questions

1. What do honeybees eat?
2. How do honeybees make honey?
3. How do bees protect themselves?

Index